Guild Press of Indiana, Inc.

Indianapolis, Indiana

When I Was Young in Indiana

a Country Life

by

Dorothy Strattan Hinshaw

Dorothy Strattan Hinshaw

**Illustrations by
Jenny E. Hinshaw**

Copyright © 1993 Dorothy Strattan Hinshaw

All rights reserved. No part of this book may be reproduced or transmitted in any form or by any means electronic or mechanical, including photocopying, recording, or by any informational storage and retrieval system, without permission in writing from the Publisher.

Guild Press of Indiana, Inc.
6000 Sunset Lane
Indianapolis, IN 46208

Printed in the United States of America

Library of Congress
Catalogue Card Number
93-081251

ISBN 1-878208-38-1

This book is for our grandchildren.

I would like to thank Jenny Hinshaw for her illustrations; Edwin Hinshaw who wrote the study guide; family members, and those relatives who still live on the family farm.

1935  **1935**

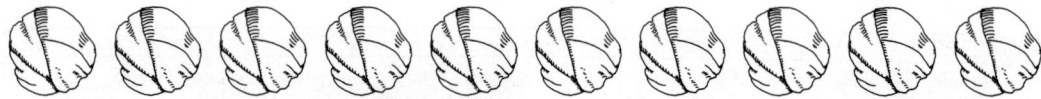

It would seem that my family had lived in Indiana forever. My Strattan grandparents lived down the road in the next farmhouse. My grandfather was a big man, but Grandmother was very small. Grandfather's name was Albert. To many younger people, this sounds like an old man. Grandfathers always seem to be so old. I remember my grandmother the most.

Albert and Louisa Strattan

Everyone called my grandmother Louie, short for Louisa. She often sat in a very small rocking chair reading the newspaper. I imagine she sat in this chair when she made rag balls. One of my games was to toss the rag balls up the stairs and watch them bounce back down. I did this again and again. They were soft and safe to throw in the house.

    Outside the house was a big grassy lawn with maple trees. Near the barn was a big water tank for the animals. The horses and cows would come for many cool drinks on hot summer days. When I was small I used to get into the water tank to cool off! Clean spring water ran into the tank, and it was the best drinking water for miles around. A tin cup always was handy for our family, neighbors, and thirsty travelers.

    The horses that drank from the water tank were named Daisy and Beauty. When Beauty grew old, she was the ugliest horse on the farm. They worked very hard pulling wagons and plows and the manure spreader. Phew! Sometimes I was allowed to ride on one of these horses as they pulled a wagon. Later, I had a regular riding horse. Much later when I was in college, I sold the horse to buy a car!

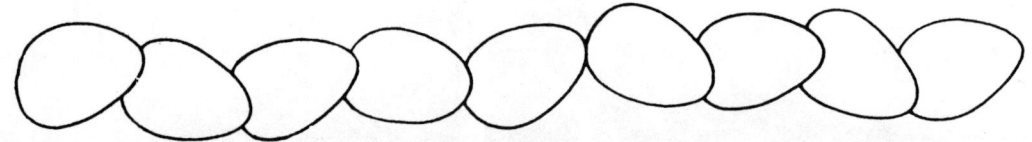

    The same spring water that watered the animals also fed into grandmother's house. She had a special room which was like a natural refrigerator. Spring water flowed into the room in a little stream. Water ran around the room in a trough. Containers of food and milk were placed on rocks in the very cold water. The spring water was also piped into the kitchen for drinking and cooking. Grandmother had a bathroom with plumbing in her house, but at our house, we had an outhouse. The outhouse was some

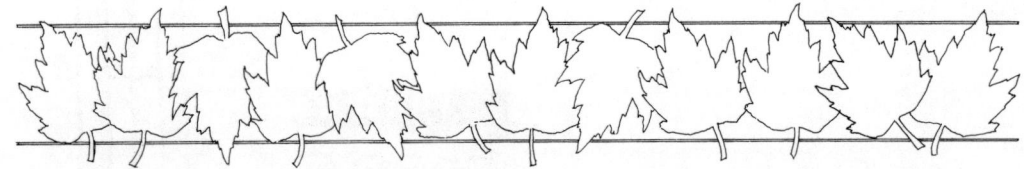

distance from the house. It was a cold, dark walk on a winter's night! We had a big round metal tub for Saturday night baths in the warmest room of the house: the dining room!

    In the Spring, I enjoyed eating maple sugar cookies. Grandma made them from the big old sugar maple trees in

our woods. Wooden buckets collected the sap and Grandfather and Dad boiled it in a big kettle in the shed until it was thick and sugary. Grandmother pressed it and made nice designs with a cookie cutter. Yum! Yum!

It was a real treat to visit my Grandmother Johnson in town. Her name was Matilda but most people called her Tillie. My grandfather, Josiah Johnson, died before I was

born. I enjoyed taking a bath in Grandmother's tub which had hot running water. I also enjoyed riding my tricycle on the sidewalk. Grandmother Johnson had an ice box instead of a spring cooled room. A big block of ice kept the food cold. I remember that Grandmother made people laugh with jokes and stories. She taught elocution, and memorized many stories that she told on special occasions. When she was too old to live alone, she came to live with us on the farm. We had a lot of fun together. One of her favorite games was "Flinch."

"Tillie" Johnson

On our farm we had our own gas well. We had many crops, such as corn, oats, soybeans, wheat, tomatoes, and peas. We had more hogs than cattle. Once a year we went to the big city thirty miles away to sell hogs and to shop. Sometimes we even went to a movie!

    When I was very young, no one in our neighborhood had television. We listened to stories on the radio and read a lot of books. I played outside in the woods, and rode my bicycle to the neighbor's houses. Or we would have visitors. Or go visiting. Or I would play with my dolls and the rag balls.

    Sometimes our whole family would sit on our front porch. We would rush out hoping to get a seat on the glider. We watched birds and animals, crops, traffic, and weather. The most exciting weather was lightning and thunder. Sheet lightning was fascinating. Streak lightning was frightening. We had some fierce storms in Indiana. Once a terrible tornado blew down my sister's garage!

♡ ♡♡♡ ♡♡ ♡♡ ♡♡ ♡

    My sister, Marilyn June, was ten years older. I could not understand why I was not allowed to accompany her on her dates with her boyfriend. But she was a good pal most of the time and I had fun visiting her in college. One time my mother played a trick on her. Mother thought her boyfriend had stayed long enough, so she lowered an alarm clock down from the upstairs heating duct into the living room and it went off in their faces!

Marilyn June and Dorothy Ellen

    My sister married a farmer and I helped my brother-in-law and my father on the farm. When I was old enough, I drove the tractor and helped put hay in the hayloft. Here is how they did this: A wagon of hay would be driven into the barn. A rope on a pulley had giant hooks which would grab the hay, and a horse or tractor would drive away from the barn pulling the giant hooks of hay up into the hayloft. Back and forth went the tractor pulling up the hay.

    I could drive a tractor and a jeep before I learned to drive a car.

Can you guess what noises I heard when I was young? Squealing pigs, mooing cows, crickets, locusts, farm machinery, the piano, and the sewing machine. When Mother was not practicing the piano, crocheting, knitting, or tatting, she sewed. Sometimes she made dresses from flowered feed sacks (ask your grandma what these were). My dad was a good mechanic and often worked on the farm machinery, took care of the animals, and planted and harvested crops. He often worried about the weather.

Eunice Lucille, Dorothy Ellen, and John Myron Strattan

My parents, grandparents, and their parents and cousins and aunts and uncles and almost everyone in my family were Quakers (Religious Society of Friends). Many of my ancestors came from North Carolina. They stopped in Indiana because they found very good farm land and plenty of water from rivers and springs. After the first migrants settled, other family members and their friends came to join them. Many Quakers formed communities and started schools and Meetings (churches). Before public schools were established, Quakers had academies for their children and any other children in the community. Later, these schools became public schools. My grandmother taught in the one-room brick schoolhouse located on our farm and my dad was a pupil.

My family went to Friends Meeting every Sunday (First Day) and brought guests home for dinner. The guest was usually a visiting elder or minister. I remember listening to funny stories my family and the guests told around the dinner table.

Knightstown Friends Meeting

Mother spread the dinner table with roast pork or beef, roasted potatoes, Waldorf salad (with marshmallows!), and scalloped corn. Often we had creamed peas in tart shells, and we always had a fresh homemade pie for dessert.

Sometimes Mother would kill and dress a chicken on Saturday for Sunday dinner!

My dad and my sister and her family.

I used to go to church camp in the summer. We had to drive many miles to the lake in northern Indiana. I made lots of friends at camp who came from all over Indiana and Ohio. One of the campers I met went to the same college I attended in Richmond, Indiana. We became good chums in college and later we were married. He is also a Quaker from Indiana!

Winter fields

and lawn

My car and I, 1954.

Riding at college.

Summer

When I was young in Indiana, I used to hear stories about my mother and father when they were young in Indiana. Do your parents have stories to tell about long ago?